A TIME OF WAR
Memoir of a Vietnam Medic

A TIME OF WAR
Memoir of a Vietnam Medic

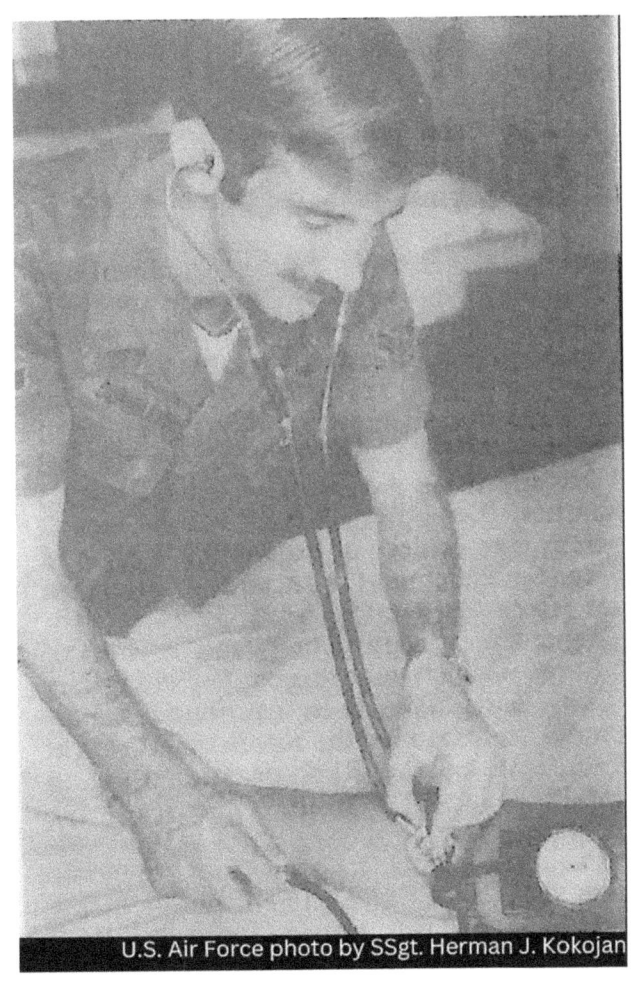

U.S. Air Force photo by SSgt. Herman J. Kokojan

Dennis L. Copenhaver
Captain, USAF, Retired

ARPress
ILLUMINATING IDEAS
EMPOWERING VOICES

ARPress
45 Dan Road Suite 5
Canton MA 02021
Hotline: 1(888) 821-0229
Fax: 1(508) 545-7580

Ordering Information:
Quantity sales. Special discounts are available on quantity purchases by corporations, associations, and others. For details, contact the publisher at the address above.

Printed in the United States of America.

ISBN-13:   Softcover   979-8-89389-616-9
                eBook   979-8-89389-617-6

Library of Congress Control Number: 2024921519

TABLE OF CONTENTS

To everything there is a season, a time for every purpose under heaven:

A time to be born, and a time to die

A time to plant, and a time to pluck what is planted

A time to kill, and a time to heal

A time to break down, and a time to build up

A time to weep, and a time to laugh

A time to mourn, and a time to dance

A time to cast away stones, and a time to gather stones

A time to embrace, and a time to refrain from embracing

A time to gain, and a time to lose

A time to keep, and a time to throw away

A time to tear, and a time to sew

A time to keep silence, and a time to speak

A time to love, and a time to hate

A time of war, and a time of peace...

He has made everything beautiful in its time.

Ecclesiastes 3:1-8, 11 (New King James Bible)

INTRODUCTION

I grew up in a rural part of Pennsylvania, the son of a local farmer. My father was a World War II veteran who landed on the beaches at Normandy, then "walked, ran or crawled all the way to Berlin." He never rode on any trucks or tanks. While he was a decorated soldier, he didn't speak much about his wartime experiences until after I returned from Vietnam when I was 21 years old. Instead, he turned to a quiet life of farming. I grew up relatively poor so we had to conserve ammunition and make every shot count. My brother and I became really good shooters, keeping groundhog numbers down in our fields. He passed on to us boys his rifle training so we "could survive if we ever had to fight in a war." "I'm not training you so you can hunt, but so you can live," he would say. It was my father, the former soldier, who taught me and my brother how to hunt, fish and track game-skills that would later help keep me alive in a turbulent wartime environment. Dad went one step further than teaching us the basics: he taught us to shoot uphill, downhill, and especially at moving targets. He would roll an old tractor tire downhill with an orange painted cardboard center and we learned to hit the center with our .30-30 rifles. Later in life I became a "Class A" shooter in both skeet and trap shooting-events where you always shoot in front of moving targets, almost never directly at the clay targets.

By the time I graduated high school in 1969, the United States had been involved in the Vietnam War for six years. I had received a congressional appointment to the United States Air Force Academy where I spent two years after graduating high school. I really wanted to be a fighter pilot or at least have a chance at becoming one. By the time I left the academy, I had fallen in love with flying. Combat in a plane-versus-plane environment did not bother me, but the idea of dropping bombs did stir my conscious to question itself.

After spending 24 months at the Air Force Academy, my father got sick so I returned home to our family farm to help my parents. That's when my life changed. It turns out that being a military cadet had kept me safe from war: My draft number had been called while at the academy, but was deferred since I was in "active duty" status while a cadet. When I left, that all changed and I was once again "fair game" for the draft. It was while I was working and going to college closer to home that I received a draft letter from the United States Army. I had only been home for five months before learning I would be going to war. Since my initial number had been called only six months after reporting to the Air Force Academy, it turned out that everyone else in that same draft group was already in combat by the time I received my draft letter.

At the time, I thought I might truly be a conscientious objector and had no desire to go to war, so I developed a plan that I thought would increase my chances of surviving. I visited the local United States Air Force recruiter and enlisted as a "Medic". With so many not returning from the Vietnam War, I thought I might actually survive as an Air Force medic since I would not be out in the field as Army and Navy medics were. Still, I was aware that there is no safe place in a war zone and I might not make it home. This reality would prove itself over and over to me during my time in Vietnam.

At the time of my enlistment, people at home were in the process of realizing the U.S. would probably not "win" the war in Vietnam. Protests were getting bigger and occurring more often. Our country was splitting in two: those who supported the war and those who didn't. Even my parents were upset over how things were going. I found out later that they kept it to themselves when I was sent to Vietnam. They didn't tell anyone I was fighting in the war and they certainly didn't have a gold star- a common symbol used to show support for a soldier at war-hanging in their window.

Only two medics of about 30 in my Medical Service Specialist class at Sheppard Air Force Base were assigned as medics in Vietnam and as fate would have it, I was one of those two. By spring of 1972, I was in Vietnam at the age of 20. I went as a young man and felt like I aged 10 years in the 8 months I was there. During that time I was a medic in our Aid Station (emergency room) for a short time, worked in the post-op surgical ward for five months, and spent my last two months as the only medic in the Heroin Rehab ward. While I was sent for a 12-month tour, I only served 8 months since I was part of the 2nd wave "withdrawal" from Vietnam. We actually drew straws to see who would depart first. While it was only 8 months, it was such an intense experience that I have carried vivid memories of it all my life. Only in recent years have I told some of my stories to close friends or family.

These are my stories from my time serving at the end of the war- but probably not in consecutive order. I am 66 years old as I write this and do feel that time and memory may not be 100%, but I will tell my stories as best I can remember them. May they give insight and understanding to anyone who cares to read them. The experience did change my life, however, I did not directly volunteer, nor would I choose to do it again if I could go back in time. I remember seeing tears in my Dad's eyes, himself a WWII combat veteran, when I told him I, too, was going to war. My mother openly wept. I promised her I would not take any unnecessary chances—a promise I would later break.

ARRIVAL

We flew for hours and hours. We finally landed in Hawaii to refuel. It was night and we were allowed to stretch our legs and go up on a roof at a nearby building. The air smelled so good. It had that tropical fresh scent. After two hours, we took off again and eventually landed in Saigon, Vietnam.

When I took my first breath off the plane, I almost gagged. I had been transported to another world. The air here smelled strongly of old urine. I later learned that people in Saigon would just squat and urinate in street gutters, so the city smelled like an open sewer. We saw rats, bigger than American house cats, scurrying around in the streets as we were bussed from the airport to the U.S. military base in Saigon. I noticed that all the bus windows had chicken wire in them. The wire was meant to protect us soldiers during transport. It would help any grenades (thrown by the Vietcong or their sympathizers) bounce off of the bus' windows. *Will I ever breathe fresh air again? Will I live to feel secure again?* I wondered.

I had to push down the fear. All the while, it's constant whisper echoed in the back of my mind… Run. But I couldn't. I knew I had to stand and fight the fear, all the while wondering, "What have I gotten myself into?" I reminded myself that I was not the first combat soldier to feel this way. "Imagine what the WWII vets must have gone through, " I told myself. "You can do this. You have to- it's too late to run. " My thoughts flew to the many men who had escaped this war by fleeing to Canada. While I was now seeing why, I had never considered that as an option. It simply wasn't who I was. "Have courage," I proclaimed to myself, as I entered what was to be my new home.

"Take Your Weapon!"

Upon arriving at the base in Saigon, every soldier went through in processing. It is here that we were given our assignments and equipment- to include uniforms and weapons. I filed in line behind the other soldiers, waiting for my turn. When that time came, I held up the line. To my dismay, I was handed an M-16 and three clips of ammo. I shook my head and handed them back- twice. I explained that I am a medic and, therefore, am not required to carry a weapon.

The frustrated sergeant finally said, "Just keep it at your bed so you can help if the base is being over-run. If they call for 'Every man hit the line,' you grab your weapon and use it."

Other than when helping to defend the base, I was not required to carry the weapon.

It wasn't that I wasn't capable of using the weapon. I had trained with an M-16 and Smith & Wesson .38 revolver and was considered an "expert" marksman by the military on both. Having hunted in Pennsylvania since I was 14 years old, I felt at home with weapons- I just didn't know whether I was comfortable using one on another human being. That's much different than hunting game on a farm.

The next day when the officer in charge discovered I was "another crazy medic that refused to carry a weapon," he assigned a tall black man to stay on my right shoulder wherever I went. It was his job to keep me alive so I could help our unit if we got hit. That man stayed there for two solid months. He was by my side all day long and never had to fire a shot. One day he informed me that he was done following me around. He said I knew when to take cover and was very good at it...and he was bored. He disappeared that day and I never saw him again.

I had come to think of him as my "shadow," but would never say that out loud. I was afraid it would not sound right. In retrospect, it had been very reassuring to have him with me during that time when I was so new to the war. Little did I know that I would repay the favor to other "green" soldiers multiple times during my tour.

CANNON FIRE

I got very little sleep the first three nights. Nobody warned me about the cannon fire. The city was ringed with friendly cannons and they fired "at random" all night, every night. As loud as thunder, the big 105mm guns created a protective exploding zone around Saigon so that any approaching enemy would think twice. At least, that was the idea...but how does one sleep through cannon fire?

I tried. *"They are keeping you safe. Go to sleep,"* I would tell myself but my mind created images of men being blown to bits. By day four, I was desperate for sleep. I decided to try something: I imagined a big fat Budda sitting. He was pounding on a drum and I thought of the "booms" from the cannon fire as drum beats. I counted them like some count sheep to go to sleep. As if by a miracle, by the fourth "boom," I was drifting off to sleep. From that night on, Budda Drummer Boy saved me from exhaustion.

"It Rains Fish Here!"

Shortly after I arrived so did the monsoon rain. The dry, hot season was coming to an end and every afternoon, clouds would come in from the ocean and dump a heavy rain shower for 20-30 minutes. Then, the sun would come out, spiking the heat and humidity. It usually rained hard, so water run-off and puddles were everywhere.

One of my bunkmates who had been there several months said to me, "By tomorrow, it will be raining fish. Don't let rain water into your mouth or you'll get a mouth full of fish!"

At the time, I thought he was joking. However, while I was walking around the puddles the next day, I saw something move inside a puddle. As I began to look around, I saw movement in all the puddles. At first, I thought, "It must be some tadpoles. " Back home, in the springtime, it wasn't unusual to find tadpoles in small puddles where a frog had left its eggs a few weeks earlier. Yet, as I looked closer, I discovered that the moving creatures were actually all baby fish. Fish that were certainly not there yesterday! Heck, the water wasn't even there a few days ago...

So when I saw my bunkmate again, I excitedly asked, "How does it rain fish here?"

He started to laugh. Then others also laughed. Everyone was laughing as he turned to me and triumphantly declared, "Gotcha, rookie!"

Once the laughter died down, I gained some insight into this phenomenon: During wet seasons in Vietnam, adult fish lay eggs in the mud. Those puddles eventually dry up and the eggs lay dormant until the next monsoon season hits. The following year, when the rains come again, the eggs hatch in one day. Since it rains everyday, it appears to be raining fish!

ROCKET/MORTAR ATTACKS

When the base was under attack, sirens would sound and a Giant Voice would holler, "We are under attack—take cover!" It didn't take me long to find all the safe places to do so. By the end of my first week, I had memorized every low spot, every wall, every bunker, every foxhole, and sandbagged area. I would run to the place providing the nearest cover and dive in. I could hear the incoming rockets barraging us. They made a terrible loud "crump" sound when they hit. These weapons of destruction threw plenty of shrapnel, smoke and fire. I could feel the ground vibrate when they were close. Most attacks only lasted 20-30 minutes.

Mortars were small compared to rockets. I was told that rockets were about three feet long and four to five inches in diameter. They flew high, then fell to the earth but were not very accurate. The mortars were smaller, but our experienced enemies were pretty good at aiming them. During a mortar attack, there was less total destruction, but they were more deadly to people. A mortar launcher could "correct fire" and drop a mortar right into your foxhole. Mortar crews were typically closer to their target while rockets could be fired from further away. However, both weapons were fired using patterns that were constantly changing.

I feared the mortars more. I would watch as the second or third shot completely destroyed helicopters and aircraft. It was a powerful weapon. While their target was not usually soldiers, one could easily lose their life if they were in the line of fire. We were considered "collateral damage." Due to their proximity to the targets, our aircraft mechanics usually took more hits than the rest of us. Fortunately for us, the people firing them had a hard time hitting their targets. Had they been more accurate, we could have had a lot more injured during each attack.

During an attack, I never ran towards our enemies' main target, the flight line. I always ran away from it! I got very good at taking cover quickly. After all, I was determined to survive the war. I later met soldiers stationed in smaller towns about 25 miles outside of Saigon who got attacked everyday. They would come to "relax" at our base, and could take cover twice as fast as me. That was impressive!

While rocket and mortar attacks were quite common on base, we also had other threats, like "zappers." These "zappers" were snipers armed with AK-47s. While our base was meant to be secure, I would soon discover that there was truly no real safe place, regardless of how quickly I could "take cover."

"Take Cover... All Medics Report To The E.R."

My first assignment was in our Aid Station, a smaller Emergency Room manned by medics, where I learned to suture wounds my second day. Three other medics worked there with me. I was considered the senior ranking medic since I already had a stripe on my arm. Since I had "served" in uniform for two years as a cadet at the United States Air Force Academy in Colorado, I came out of basic training with a higher rank, designated by the stripe. The others had no stripes yet and were Airmen Basics in rank. Because of the time I spent at the academy before being drafted, I was about two years older than them as well. They usually looked up to me, but that was about to change.

One day the medics and I were returning to our barracks when the alarm sounded and rockets and mortars started to fall. Since we were not in battle gear, we didn't have helmets or flack jackets on. We were only wearing our jungle fatigues, which were void of any protective gear. Hearing the alarm, we all scooted into the nearest bunker. That's when we heard the giant voice shout, "All personnel take cover. All Medics report to the E.R."

The most outspoken of my fellows said "Let's go. We're only 300-400 yards from the E.R."

"Wait. Stand fast and let me call them," I said.

I picked up the bunker's buried phone and rang the E.R. The staff answered right away. I gave my name, location, and number of medics before asking, "How many incoming wounded do you have?"

"None at this time.

I told him to ring the bunker if there were any incoming wounded and we would report. Otherwise, we would stay here in sight of the E.R., where we were safe.

I hung up and told the other medics to "stand fast" (remain in place) as we heard the thunder of enemy weapons falling around us.

Again, the overzealous medic said, "You are never going to get any medals that way."

"Why run through a barrage of fire to go help when there are no wounded yet? You may end up the first hit or killed. Stay here- and that's an order," I barked. "I outrank you all and if anyone does not like my decision, I will take responsibility for it."

"Screw you. I'm going," he responded.

He talked the other two into going with him. Knowing I wasn't going to change their mind, I asked them to space themselves out. I feared that if they ran as a group, they would all three get hit by the same rocket. He started to leave and the other two medics immediately followed him.

They quickly caught up with the first man and then ran side-by-side with me hollering at them, "No. Spread out, damn it!"

It could have been a disaster, but somehow they made it to the E.R. untouched. I called the E.R. and advised them that three medics were on their way after disobeying my direct order.

In the aftermath, I was ordered to report to our commander, who was a Colonel. I was waiting my turn to see him, but could hear him hollering at the other three medics for being stupid and not staying under cover until needed. He proceeded to really let them have it for disobeying a direct order from me.

Then my turn came. He smiled and thanked me for trying to keep my men alive. As it turned out, it was a blessed day. Nobody got hit and there were no wounded to care for that day. My commander and I both thanked God that our medics were not killed.

Months later, we were all sent home. My fellow medics got disciplined several times-and subsequently received no medals. They had thought I was a coward that day. I was not. I just wanted us all to live to go home, if possible.

MY CROSS: A SIGN OF FAITH

I decided to wear a cross around my neck, I shortened my dog tag chain so that this small cross showed at my neck in the front. It was not just "bling" as they call it today. It was telling the world that I believe in Jesus Christ. The cross was an inch wide and 13/4 inches tall and appeared to be made of silver. I had bought it at a street side vendor stand in Saigon. I probably paid too much for it, but we always negotiated a lower price than the vendor first asked for. Whatever I ended up paying, it was worth it. The cross was beautiful and very shiny- and was now my newest uniform addition.

From the day I bought it, I never took it off. Technically, that meant I was out of uniform. This wasn't uncommon in our war zone though. I saw soldiers with long hair tucked under their caps and many other uniform violations. I wasn't trying to be rebellious, I simply needed something to remind me to be strong and that there was One greater than the pain and suffering of this war. So, I waited to see what would happen, but nobody said anything to me about violating our uniform code- not even a one-star general. They say there are no atheists in foxholes. In fact, I think everyone felt that we needed all the help we could get. "Add a prayer for me, would you Cope?" my fellow soldiers often requested upon seeing the symbol of faith at the base of my neck.

I wore this cross until I got home to the farm in Pennsylvania. By that time it was turning my neck green. Yet, I knew that this little symbol of something so much bigger had helped me tremendously while in Vietnam. By the time I took it off, all the silver had worn off- or was sweated off in the tropical heat- leaving only copper underneath. It now looked the same color as an old penny. It used to be so pretty with the sparkling silver on it, and was now just an ugly, dull piece of copper.

In many ways, that cross was much like us soldiers: beautiful when new with a bit of ugliness underneath that wouldn't be revealed until we went to war. I saw people at their best and at their worst. I was ashamed of the way my fellow Americans treated "other" people. We used them- even enslaved them. During the war, women were sold to GIs for a price- sometimes even by their own relatives. I had never seen slavery before. It was shocking: the women seemed to accept their fate and worked hard for their owner's comfort and pleasure. I came to realize that most of them were desperate for a way to survive, but that did not make taking advantage of them, right. How quick humanity reverts to pagan ways. In many ways, that old cross was a reminder to me that it is what's inside that counts when you're dealing with people.

I threw my wartime jewelry away thinking that nobody would ever wear it again, but years later I wish I had kept it to remind me of what we are all made of. When I think about that cross, I will always be reminded that Jesus shines us up like sterling silver- and that he is the only one who can.

WHAT'S ON THE FENCE?

I got up one morning, walked to the back of our "houch" (barracks- our living quarters) and stood on the back step. It wasn't a place I would normally go, but for some reason I chose to start my morning there that day.

My body ached. Sleeping on such a small cot was making my young bones ache. By now, I should have been used to sleeping in the standard twin sized metal-framed bunk bed. Each night we were enclosed in a mosquito net and a small oscillating fan made it cool enough to sleep in just underwear. We quickly learned never to touch the net with any part of our bodies or we would wake up with that body part covered with itchy mosquito bites. Sleep would have been impossible without those nets.

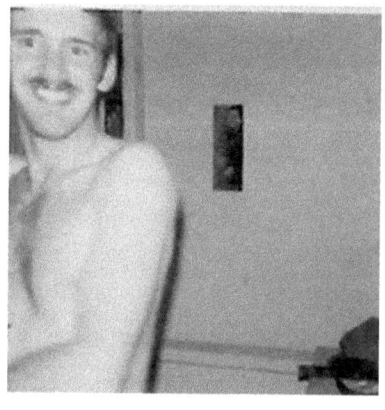

Still trying to wake up, I rubbed my eyes, yawning as I attempted to stretch through the aches and pains of another long night. As my eyes focused, I saw something on the inner perimeter fence, less than 100 yards away from where I was standing. I stepped back inside and asked to borrow another soldier's binoculars. I gasped when the image came into focus. It was a bomb wired to the fence- our protective barrier on the inside perimeter of the base! I could clearly see 12 sticks of TNT attached to an old fashioned wind-up clock being used as a detonator.

We called the security police and they sent over the bomb disposal unit. Whoever set the bomb had wound the spring too tight and it broke, so it didn't go off! A bomb that size would have flattened our houch and God knows how many others. The security police confirmed that it was likely the detonator that had broken by mistake. Our enemies were trying to scare and harass us. The Vietcong were sending us a message: *We are still here.* Nobody knew how they had gotten inside the perimeter fence and back out without being seen, but the knowledge that they'd been there confirmed one thing:

There was no safe area- not even on the biggest and safest base we had.

THE CONSCIENTIOUS OBJECTOR

I went to Vietnam thinking I was a conscientious objector. That's why I refused to carry a weapon. I had been told that a conscientious objector "would not kill to save his or her own life or the lives of the wounded that they are treating."

At the time I was drafted for war, my mind had gone through the options available to me. I had considered running to Canada, but knew if I did that I would never be able to face my father again. He was a World War II combat veteran. Thinking about it made my stomach turn. My father had been a rifleman and bazooka man for a 120-man unit, but only 20 of them lived to see Berlin captured.

So, I had chosen to become an Air Force medic (our official title at the time was a Medical Service Specialist). I figured that, in this role, I would probably stay out of the jungle and rice patties, and have a higher chance of survival. I was halfway through my time in Vietnam when I learned something very important about myself...

I had gone to the base exchange to get my hair trimmed and buy a few personal items. I was crossing a big paved area on my way back to my houch when suddenly a mortar hit close to the helicopter pad. Then, mortars started to fall all around me- fast and furious. It was 500 yards or more to the nearest bunker and the mortars were falling in between me and the one place where I could potentially take cover. One fell too close for comfort and I dropped to the ground. I had no intention of getting back up and getting cut in half. I maintained the position I fell in. I deliberately wanted to appear dead, hoping that any zapper or mortar crew would not waste ammo on a dead man.

Pieces of asphalt fell on me and I could see some of the fireballs as they exploded. Thank God, no bullets were also flying. There seemed to be just one enemy mortar crew, probably in the trees located about 600 yards from me. Then I noticed that, starting back towards the tree line, mortars were walking closer and closer towards me. Playing possum on the tarmac, I kept thinking that the next one would probably land right on top of me...and then I'll be gone.

I should have been praying for them to stop. Instead, I was thinking If the shooters are in that patch of trees they are in range of my M- 16... If only I had it with me. I glanced around. There wasn't anyone near me, so there was no chance of using someone else's weapon either. I was all alone and found myself wanting to fight back. I remember thinking, I can't take this. Someone give me a gun and I'll stop them- even if I have to kill them in order to make them stop aiming for me. I asked myself if I would really put bullets in the men shooting at me. The answer was, Yes.

What do you know... I wasn't a conscientious objector after all. I absolutely hated being a target. I had just enough time to think, God forgive me, then it got deadly quiet. No more mortars were falling around me, but I wasn't about to move until I heard the "All Clear" from the Loud Voice. Yet, even hearing that could not stop the pounding of my anxious heart. I sat up and looked around. My heart raced as I saw huge impact holes on three sides of me.

I learned much about myself that day- some of which surprised me. I now knew that I was never a conscientious objector. I just hadn't lived through a real life or death situation before. As I returned to the barracks, I wondered what Jesus thought of me now. I felt like I finally knew what Peter felt like when he tried to walk on water. Fear does something to all of us.

WORKING SICK CALL

Our Aid Station had a sick call every morning. The soldiers we attended to were divided into two groups, "V.D." and "not V.D." We were categorizing based on what soldiers called "The Clap", a sexually transmitted disease also known as gonorrhea.

I was told to give shots to the men who tested positive, as determined by seeing the bacteria under a microscope. I asked how many shots to prepare. It took four shots per patient so I was told to prepare two cases. We treated 15-25 men every day and some were in every week to be retreated.

When treating soldiers, I would ask them, "One sexual partner or several?"

I discovered that the repeat patients were actually men living with a Vietnamese partner. I told my Sergeant that we couldn't cure them unless we were willing to treat their partners/ wives. So, I started a back-door clinic where these men brought their partners in so I could treat both of them at once. Within a few weeks, I only needed one case of injectors every morning.

It was a terrible problem and it did not make me eager to risk relations with the local women.

WOUNDED BY ACCIDENT

I was working in our Aid Station where it was our job to take care of the "walking wounded" – those with lacerations or other non-life-threatening wounds. It was here, on my second day, that I learned how to suture wounds.

One day, we heard the siren go off, signaling we were under attack. Shortly thereafter, an ambulance came in with three stretcher patients. Each stretcher was carried by two men. They came rushing in, shouting "make a hole" as they came down a narrow hall. Feeling that I was in their way, I leaped backwards against a wall to make room for them. The walls of our Aid Station were normally lined with clean urinals and bedpans, held in place by brackets. As I leaped back, I felt something very sharp pierce my clothing and penetrate my back until it was stopped by something hitting my ribs. My back had come into contact with a broken bracket on the wall. Pulling myself off of the dagger-like piece of metal, I felt something warm running down my back.

The broken bracket was dripping my blood.

I proceeded to help take care of the wounded men, even sewing one back up. When we were finished, the Sergeant declared, "Okay. We're done."

"Not yet," I said, taking off my blood-stained shirt and turning so he could see my back. "Would someone please sew me up?"

I pointed to the bracket which was still dripping my blood. They laid me down and Sarge sewed me up.

"One inch up or down and your lung would have collapsed," he told me. "Your rib saved you.... Oh, by the way," he said. "Would you like me to put you in for a Purple Heart?"

"Don't you dare dishonor our wounded like that," I indignantly replied. "That bracket is not a piece of shrapnel and my injury was accidental. This is not a combat related wound."

He agreed- and I never earned a Purple Heart. I was quite glad of that, considering the experiences soldiers go through who are awarded them. Many of them lost limbs or an eye. Some spent many months in rehab and many never returned to active duty. By the end of the war, over 50,000 American soldiers had died from their wounds.

While my back carried a scar for years, it was not combat-related. Later, when my sister asked me to tell her about being wounded, I told her the truth, but she didn't believe me. She stormed away mad because she thought I was lying to her.

HOW I SPENT MY DAYS OFF

I decided to do something positive on my only day off each week, which happened to be Sundays. I went to morning services at our base chapel and spoke to several other Christians there. One of them asked, "Have you met the Baptist preacher in Saigon?" When I told him I hadn't, he volunteered to take me to meet him.

We rode the bus to the church "compound", as they called it. The front of the compound faced the street and looked like the Alamo in San Antonio, Texas. The first thing I noticed was the wall around it. The stone wall was topped with concertina wire and broken beer bottles. The necks of the bottles were actually cemented into the top of the wall, creating razorblade sharp spikes made of glass. Anyone going over that wall would have needed special assault gear to make it unscathed. Outside the wall perimeter, a Vietnamese civilian armed with an M-16 and side arm protected the compound. The gate to the compound remained locked except to let people in and out. Inside the compound, a second armed security guard patrolled the interior wall perimeter. I had never before seen a church with this kind of security.

The preacher was a snow-white haired gentleman with no sign of balding who wore his wavy hair rather long. He was married to a blonde woman who was taller than him. While the Preacher was probably in his forties, possibly pushing 50, his wife was a bit younger than him. The couple had two tall, blonde teenagers: a boy and a girl. Quite a likeable fellow, I quickly became fond of the Preacher and his family. It was surprising to me that he had his family with him in a war zone. That was something the military didn't allow.

I told my preacher friend that I was off on Sundays and asked him if there was anything I could do to help him. "Work with the young people to help them become fluent in English. I can't convert them if I can't talk to them," he told me. So I did. It took several months, but their conversational English progressed rapidly with practice. Soon, all of them could read and write English better than Americans who were the same age. I was really impressed with that. I started with about 20 students, but ended up with 30 in just a few weeks.

When working with them, I was given some basic ground rules: never say anything bad about Ho Chi Minh, the Vietcong or our other enemies. To do so would result in an empty classroom. I was told that if I did, from that day on, my students would fear that satchel charges would be thrown over the wall from passing motor scooters. All it would take is for one student to be an observer for the Vietcong- then my class would disappear. Therefore, I never talked about the war.

My class and I learned a lot about each other's countries and cultures during our time together. We enjoyed sharing in English, of course. "You tell me something about your country and I will tell you about mine," I'd say to start the conversation. Then we would ask each other questions. We did more formal things in class as well, but I found that they relaxed in this more conversational setting. They also didn't seem to mind when I asked them to repeat themselves, just so I could get them to speak English like people back home. I suppose if you run into any Vietnamese natives with Pennsylvania accents, it may be my fault.

I was a serious teacher who spoke his best college level English with my students. I only remember one student who never seemed to improve. The rest did extremely well. Sadly, there were no boy students over the draft age of 18 in my class. They all had to serve in the Vietnamese military or go to college. I did have some older girls in my class, though, since females were exempt from the draft. I found that my boy students worked really hard, as their future would depend on how well they could speak English when interviewed.

I was ordered to stop teaching during my last two weeks in Vietnam. It became too dangerous to go into Saigon once the Vietnamese knew the U.S. military was leaving. However, I still made two more trips to the Preacher's compound. During my first trip, I begged the Preacher to take his family and leave Vietnam. I told him that we knew the North Vietnamese and Vietcong were massing around the city again. One week later, he sent his wife and kids back to the U.S., but refused to leave. I made the second trip to see him several weeks later. At that time, I looked him in the eye and said, "If you stay here, you will die here. Your wife and kids will then be on their own." I was told, and I hope it is true, that the Preacher left on a civilian aircraft the day before I left Vietnam. I thanked the Lord when I heard that news.

I Break My Promise To My Mother

This is probably one of the most vivid memories of Vietnam. There were certainly times when I felt tested- by God, circumstance, or fate. On this day, there was another rocket attack in mid-afternoon. I had my jungle fatigues on but no protective gear. I always carried at least one bandage in my thigh pocket. That's all I had with me. Immediately after the attack started, I made it to a foxhole with sandbags around the top. I was all by myself. Looking up from the foxhole, I noticed that the surrounding area was flat and mostly paved. I will be safe, I thought, unless there is a direct hit into the foxhole.

Then I heard it- a man screaming like his insides were torn out. I peeked over the sand bags. There he was, about 100 yards away, rolling from side to side and clutching his head- and screaming again and again. I was confused because no rockets had landed close to us. Then I thought, "zappers" (sniper!). I reminded myself that I was a medic and it was my job to go get him. I would stop the bleeding- or die trying, I told myself.

Remember, I never carried a weapon so I could not shoot back at zappers. I would have to risk my life to save him, but I realized that nobody else could see us or hear him. As I considered staying in place where I was safe, the sound of his screams forced me to shake the fear off. I could not be a coward and let him die alone.

The last thought through my head was, "I'm sorry mom, I just have to do this." So out I went as low and fast as I could crawl. I felt the ground shake with rocket impacts. I covered my head when dirt and chips of pavement fell on me. I finally made it to his side.

When I grabbed his arm and spoke to him, he just kept screaming like he could not hear me. I did not see any blood so I pounded his arm and shouted, "Stop screaming," as loud as I could. After about three times, he suddenly realized I was there and stopped.

"Now look at me!" I made him lock his eyes on mine. "Where are you hit?" I asked.

"What?"

I repeated myself.

"I'm not hit. I'm just scared!"

I'm not sure what curse word I said, but it was followed by, "You're going to get us both killed!"

Then another rocket hit close. I shouted, "Follow me to the fox hole."

"I can't. I can't move."

"Yes you can! Give me your hand. Now grab hold tight to my pant leg and when I say move... move your ass, soldier," I said in my best drill instructor voice.

I dragged him the first ten feet or so, but then he discovered it was less painful to crawl and that he could move. I pulled him into the foxhole, threw him up against the side and covered him with my body. We did not move until the "All Clear" sounded. Then, I sat back and finally looked at him. He was a black soldier, about 6' 2" who was built like a linebacker. He was dressed in a khaki uniform, not fatigues, and he had no protective gear on.

Staring at him, I asked "How long have you been in country?"

"About twenty minutes."

"Did you go through basic training?"

"Yes."

I asked him if he had practiced "taking cover" and he said he had.

"If you want to see your mother again, you must do the things you were trained to do without thinking! We are all scared and you should be but promise me you won't give them a target to shoot at!"

"I won't," he replied.

He thanked me for not leaving him exposed and alone. Then we went our separate ways. I never saw him again. We had not even asked each other what our names were. It did not matter. I hope he remembers me...if he lived to go home.

TENDING THE WOUNDED

The wounded stayed in our post-op surgical ward until they were stable enough for the long flight home. What follows are a few of the stories that stand out during the six months I worked there...

"I Speak French"

Our surgical ward consisted of a multi-national staff: South Vietnamese, Americans, and South Korean soldiers worked together to treat our wounded. Our patients included allied soldiers from all of these countries and sometimes the leading Registered Nurse was from another nation. Working with other nations brought many challenges. Not only were there cultural differences, but sometimes there were barriers to communication as well...

On one occasion, I was assisting a 40-year-old Vietnamese nurse who didn't speak English. I didn't speak Vietnamese either, which normally was not a problem since most of the soldiers I worked with spoke English. However, on occasion, I found myself in more complicated situations like this.

As we worked on a wounded South Vietnamese soldier together, suddenly, blood began to spurt from his chest. He had an arterial bleed. The nurse began to frantically look through her instruments but couldn't find what she needed. She threw an instrument back onto the medical cart- and started cursing. I was shocked that I understood what she was saying. This nurse was swearing in French, not Vietnamese. I had studied French for four years in high school and even took one year of it in college. I knew enough of the language to be able to read magazines written in French.

Getting excited, I shouted to her in French, "Hey, I speak French! Tell me what you need and I will go and get it." She replied in French. I got the instrument, she clamped the bleeder and we saved the soldier's life!

Over the next month, we only spoke in French to each other, ignoring the funny looks we received from everyone who overheard us. I learned that she was taught French when France had occupied her nation years ago. She was pleasant to work with and I enjoyed practicing my French with her. It was a nice escape from some of the horror we encountered each day.

"Please Kill Me"

We had several patients who had been burned by our own Napalm bombs. One or two of them had directed the strike right to their own location because they felt they would not survive the attack.

They had been surrounded in combat and calling the strike was their last effort to survive. While it had worked, it also left them as casualties of war.

One American soldier had been paralyzed from the neck down. He used to whisper to me when we were alone, "Cope, please just kill me. Don't send me home like this... Just use the pillow." This soldier felt that he was worthless and was now just waiting for death. He had given up all hope. The idea of his family seeing him like this, or the burden that caring for him would bring to

them, was simply too much for him to bear. He must have begged me at least twelve times to end his life, either by overdose or using the pillow. Unfortunately, we had no antidepressants to give our patients either. After telling him I couldn't help him that way and that it was against my beliefs, he was shipped home to the U.S.

"Liar"

Not everyone was as pleasant to work with as the Vietnamese nurse. An American nurse that I worked with overheard me tell one of my colleagues that I had attended the United States Air Force Academy in Colorado Springs, Colorado for a few years. She later chewed me out for lying. She also made derogatory comments about enlisted members of the military not being smart enough to earn degrees. I informed her that the other medic working with me had three college degrees. With this kind of education, he could have easily received a commission into the military as an officer, but he hadn't wanted the responsibility that came with it in a wartime environment.

When this nurse found a yearbook from the USAF Academy that contained a photo of me during my second year there, she later apologized. I accepted her apology, but asked her to begin treating all of her medics better-especially the young man with three degrees.

"Was That My Foot?"

One day I was assigned to change dressings on an American lieutenant's foot. He had stepped too close to a mine and it had detonated. This lieutenant had begged the doctors not to amputate his foot since he wanted to go back to leading his unit. He was afraid losing a limb would end his military career and knew he was risking his life by not allowing the operation since he could easily die from sepsis or gangrene.

When he entered our ward, his foot appeared to be dying which I feared would lead to a life threatening condition. I was the only one working with him at the time and I told him that I did not want him to die from this condition. I remember thinking, He is so brave, but I could smell his foot and was very concerned. For two days, I examined the foot only to report "no pulses", a sign that no blood was getting to the foot. It was merely dead tissue now, leaving the patient at very high risk for gangrene. So, I asked a doctor to check it but he never came. Perhaps a more urgent need prevented him from appearing that day.

On the third day, I came back to change the bandages again. As I took the dressings off, the foot fell off and rolled across the floor! Hearing the thump, the lieutenant turned to me and asked, "Was that my foot?" His face revealed surprise but showed me that he didn't feel any pain. I quickly covered his leg since the tendons were hanging out, looking a lot like spaghetti. I then found the nurse on duty. I was too grossed out to eat lunch that day, so I skipped the meal being served: spaghetti.

"You, No! I Do"

We had most of a South Korean unit come in at one time. They told me their story through gestures: They had walked into a well-planned ambush by the Vietcong. They knew that if they charged the ambush, they had to run through a minefield. They did just that. They had volunteered one at a time to lead the way. If one man stepped on a mine, the next man went. They had been willing to sacrifice themselves to clear a path- and they did. The unit had run through and wiped out the Vietcong enemy that day. Their sacrifice could be seen throughout our ward: We had four or five men without a leg or two, one without an arm, and another half dozen had other injuries.

These men were fierce warriors. Even the Vietcong usually would not stand and fight them. We called them "ROKs" (pronounced 'rocks'), which was short for their home nation: Republic of Korea. They were our friends in this war. As soldiers who were trained not to show pain, they never cried out from distress, but I quickly learned to detect when they needed pain meds. When they arrived in our ward, I had to convince them to remove their gory souvenirs from their battle with the Vietcong. They had come in wearing strings of human ears.

Even though they were in a recovery ward, their sergeant would make them do morning exercises everyday...until he was ordered to stop. We had a Korean doctor working in our unit, so I let him give orders to the ROK soldiers. He was an officer and they obeyed him.

One day, a ROK soldier with one leg refused to use the urinal and kept looking at me and pointing to the bathroom. Suddenly, I felt a tap on my shoulder and turned around. Standing there was the man with one arm.

He firmly said to me, "You, no. I do!"

Putting his only arm around the man with one leg, he helped him hop to the restroom to stand and pee like a man. Then, he helped him come back. I wish I'd had a camera in that moment. I could have had a Pulitzer Prize winning photo. I can still close my eyes and see this happen.

I remember thinking to myself, *God help us is we ever have to fight these people.*

"Major Mom"

Our Registered Nurses were the only American women I ever saw in Vietnam. Our oldest nurse, who was probably in her forties, was a Major. The Major was a pleasant person who was always smiling. Since most of our patients were nineteen or twenty years old, she endearingly referred to them as "my boys". When one of the wounded patients heard this, he began calling her "mom". The nickname stuck.

From then on, our head nurse was referred to as "Mom" or "Major Mom" by our patients. The medics called her "Major," especially when outsiders were on the floor. However, when we needed her, we'd often tell another colleague to "go get Mom for me." As I write this today, I realize that even after 33 years of working with nurses throughout my career, she is still the best nurse I have ever worked with. As a wartime medic, I was her assistant in the surgical post-op unit. It was a role I enjoyed, especially since she always took on the very toughest cases...

One day we were sent a severely injured young soldier who was the same age as one of Major Mom's children back home. While this man survived his wounds, it was days before he actually started to recover. I assisted Mom each day in changing his bandages as we tried to keep him comfortable so he could gain his strength back.

On this particular day, the wounded soldier was in severe pain, and by all indications, close to death. Mom's hands were moving quietly and very precisely, but gently. Suddenly, her hands stopped and I knew something was wrong. I glanced at the injured soldier, but he looked stable. Then I glanced at Mom who was leaning forward to check his wounds. She remained silent as her eyes began brimming with tears. Soon the glasses she was wearing were so full of tears that she could no longer see. I snapped off my gloves and said, "Major, Look at me, please." I reached up to remove her glasses. After cleaning and drying them, I put them back on her face. She nodded at me, thanking me silently with her eyes. Her hands started flying again as she put new dressings on the soldier. I, too, put a fresh pair of gloves on and got back to work.

I never told anyone about her tears, but I honestly felt her real love for "her boys" as I watched her help them survive and heal. If she still lives, I hope she reads this as I never got to tell her what she meant to all of us. She would be in her eighties now.

In looking back, I realize that our unit did something remarkable, In the six months I was part of the surgical post-op unit, all of our wounded survived and were air evacuated back to their homes or to a recovery unit in the U.S. While we averaged about twenty severely wounded per week, we did not lose a single soldier. This was quite a miracle, considering the war we were fighting, but I did not realize it at the time. They all went home- something I contribute to Major Mom's leadership and example of compassion.

God bless you and keep you, Major Mom.

"I'M NOT AFRAID- I REFUSE TO BE SCARED."

We had a medical supply man in our houch. He seemed to be getting more and more frustrated with every attack. We were all taking cover in our houch one day during a rather close hail of mortars.

Suddenly, he jumped up and shouted, "I've had it! I'm not afraid of those SOB's- I refuse to be scared."

He threw off his helmet and flack jacket, stripped off his clothes, threw a towel over his shoulder and shouted, "It's time for my shower and that's what I'm going to do."

His eyes were wild and crazy. We all watched as this naked man left the building and walked at a slow, deliberate pace to the shower building 50 yards away.

The man beside me said, "Cope, we've got to go get him or he'll be killed."

"No," I said. "He's already halfway there and he is not in the mood to listen to us. If we go, we could all be killed."

And so we waited, holding our breath every time we heard an explosion. Finally, the man emerged, wet from his shower. We watched in amazement as he walked through the barrage again, his bare chest glistening in the sun, towel wrapped around his waist...and singing to himself. The sirens continued to wail in warning, as he made his way back to our houch.

When he arrived, there wasn't a scratch on him. He just sat on the edge of his bed, looked directly at us and said, "Sorry guys, but I'm just tired of being scared." Then he laid back and was asleep by the time the "All-Clear" sounded.

BLACK MARKET AND THE ENEMY

Nobody told us about the "Black Market." I learned the hard way. A soldier in the medical supply company asked me what I thought about "something." He wanted my opinion on an issue: He had been approached by a Vietnamese individual who had offered him $100 U.S. dollars for every unit of plasma he could get his hands on. This soldier had figured out how to fudge his orders so that he could skim whole cases of plasma to sell on the Vietnamese Black Market. Of course, these supplies ended up in our enemy's hands. Enemy wounded soldiers were now being treated with supplies paid for by American tax payers' money. Money, in the hands of our enemy, also came from bodies of dead American G.I.s or profits from businesses in Saigon...all kinds of businesses.

The supply soldier stood to "get rich" if he did not get caught. I told him I would never do anything to "aid the enemy" unless he wanted to risk jail or worse. They used to execute traitors, you know. I suggested he stop talking to me about this. I did not want to know if he decided to do it. Nor did I want to be considered part of his plan either. In fact, I told him, "Never speak to me about this again." That way I could truthfully say I only knew he was tempted, but I wouldn't know any details at all. I could then honestly say that I told him, "Don't do it."

While that was my first exposure to the Black Market in Vietnam, the issue would eventually hit closer to home. My housekeeper, who was employed to clean up the hutches the soldiers were quartered in, started to ask me to buy little things for her at the Base Exchange, our small shopping area on base. They were inexpensive, everyday use things which she only asked for a limited amount of "for her family," I said, "Okay, I'll get those things for you" and purchased them with the money she gave me. Then, one day, she asked me to buy D-Cell flashlight batteries for her. She requested about 2-4 batteries a month, but eventually requested I buy them by the case for her. When I asked her why she needed so many, she told me that the electricity goes off a lot and that she may need them after I am no longer in Vietnam getting them for her. After months of having her in my personal space, she was someone I trusted. She would clean our area, do our laundry and shine our shoes... and she never touched anything else that belonged to us while there. Not even my M-16, which was still at the head of my bed, along with three clips of ammo. I was about to learn what a trusting fool I was.

I turned 21 while in Vietnam, and decided to celebrate at the Enlisted Club, a nice bar we had on our base. I was enjoying my birthday drink when I overheard several higher ranking enlisted members, Non-commissioned Officers, talking at the table beside me. Perhaps it was the tone in the first soldiers voice that caught my attention.

"What do you think? Are they doing it on purpose? Or are they so damned ignorant that the poor dumb bastards don't know what they're doing?"

"Sure, they know" the other answered. "They just don't care. By helping the locals, they get back favors. The sad part is that the enemy is using what they buy to kill us. I hope the bastard gets killed by a rocket shot off with the batteries he sold them."

"If we catch him, he should be shot, " the other retorted.

"But maybe he doesn't know they stack the batteries in paper towel tubes and then use them to ignite and launch those damn rockets at us! Dumb bastard. I feel sorry for him."

Astonished, I quickly finished my drink and left the building. My thoughts raced as I realized how many rockets could be launched at us with the two cases of batteries I had bought for my cleaning lady.

I never bought her anything else again.

The interesting thing was that she was relatively well off with what she made from her housekeeping job. There were twelve of us in the houch and we each paid her $5/month, so she was sitting pretty with a salary of $60/month. I don't know what made her do it. Maybe she got greedy. I wondered, though, how many others she had pulled this same trick on. It made me nauseous thinking of her supplying the Vietcong with materials used to try and kill us.

I had made a terrible mistake- and it made me "grow up" real fast, like so many things I was exposed to during this war.

RACIAL TENSIONS

I grew up in a very rural area of western Pennsylvania. My schools were a mixture of white children of both white-collar and blue-collar workers, as well as some very poor farmers. Our town had no real minority population. There wasn't a single African-American or Hispanic person. There weren't even any first-generation immigrants living in my town. I had never even seen a person of color until I joined the service.

In Vietnam, we had plenty of black soldiers. They were good soldiers too. They really had each other's backs, but something still felt off to me. There was still a resounding awareness that our country was struggling with civil rights issues back home.

I've already mentioned the man assigned to keep me alive. I didn't know anything about the soldier when I heard the awful screams of the man who went down during an attack. I simply heard a soldier's agony and responded as a medic should. I crawled through the barrage to try to help him. It was a very basic principle in the military: Risk my life today knowing that tomorrow that person would be risking his for me. Yet, I noticed something was wrong within our military ranks.

I worked on one shift with a man who told me his father was black and his mother was Cherokee Indian. He was a lighter color with his mother's facial features. I went to lunch one day and saw my co-worker sitting by himself. So, I sat down next to him.

He started acting nervous and said, "Cope, What are you doin?"

"Eating lunch," I answered. "What's the matter?"

"You better leave," he informed me. "They're watching us. Go sit at another table please. "

"Are you kidding me?" I retorted. "We work together. We're friends, remember."

"But we can't be in public," he said. "They'll get mad and beat us both up. They already call me an 'oreo cookie'- black on the outside, white on the inside. That's why I sit alone. They make it clear that I'm not one of them."

"Well, I don't want you to sit all alone," I said. "I think I'll stay."

"No. You can't. Please go, or I'll have to move," he replied.

So, I moved- and ate by myself. I felt my face getting very red, as my anger at the situation rose. I hated what we were doing to each other.

A few months later, I was on a new shift with a new team. I got along well with everybody on my team. Later that month, I was out on the streets of Saigon when a group of black soldiers walked past me. I saw my co-worker. Nodding to him, I said hello. He just stared straight ahead like he did not hear me.

I saw him once again that same evening, this time stopping right in front of him. Looking him straight in the eye, I said, "How 'ya doing?"

He stepped around me, pretending not to see me once again. I was shocked! I heard one of the guys he was with say, "Hey man. He was talking to you. Do you know that Honky?"

In that moment, I realized that work place relationships and social relationships were two different things when skin tone was involved. I was being rejected socially because I was white... and it felt awful. I was finally understanding what discrimination feels like.

Shortly after this incident, I was moved to the prisoner medical unit and I never saw the man who "could not see me" again. I never could figure out what to say if I saw him again, but that never did happen.

I remember thinking that I wish my coworker had seen me bring that screaming man to my foxhole and cover him with my body. I was his only armor that day. It was a matter of life and death, and I saw no colors. What I did see was a fellow American- and a reminder that we were all under a whole lot of stress.

ALONE AND UNARMED

Halfway into my tour of duty, I decided to do something unusual. I would go visit the family of one of my students. I was teaching English to older students who could read and write English. They wrote better than U.S. high school students. They had perfect grammar, but no experience actually speaking English. Most of them wanted to go to the United States or Europe to study for college. My job was to get them up to par in speaking English. I acquired this role while working every Sunday for a Baptist preacher who was a local missionary. I met my friend at the school. She and I were the same age. She was shy, but dignified. I heard rumors that her family was wealthy and that her father was an influential man who owned a gas station.

I hired a taxi driver to take me to my friend's home in Saigon. He drove and drove and drove. It took at least twenty minutes to get there- and I saw no Americans during the last fifteen minutes. In fact, I saw no white people at all. I remember wondering, Are we even still in Saigon- maybe at its very edge? Anything outside of Saigon was Vietcong territory and unsafe. I wore my khaki uniform. I looked sharp, but it was obvious that I was unarmed.

Finally, the driver stopped. He pointed up a low-grade hill and said, "You find up there on left. You walk from here."

"No. You take me to this address," I said.

"No can do. You walk."

We both insisted. I finally resorted to getting more money out.

"No can do, GI," my driver stated, looking visibly distressed.

His voice quivered and his body shook as he spoke to me. He started Sweating badly and then I understood. He feared for his life if he went up that I cannot. I cannot." He was almost in tears when I street. He kept saying, said, "Okay" and paid him with a modest tip.

Then my heart started to pound. What am / doing? Why would a taxi driver fear the people who live here? The street was wide and made of hard clay. The buildings were two stories high and open, facing the street. Beads or cloth curtains hung where the inside walls and doors would be back home. Many people were cooking on small fires in the street. People around me were working on domestic projects in the street. I saw everything except weapons. Not one, but it did not matter.

All eyes were on me as I started up that street. People froze when they saw me. Talking ceased. Their expressions were one of sheer disbelief. Inside, I felt like turning around and running. But I kept my expression firm and tried to look determined. I watched the openings, half expecting a rifle barrel to be pointed at me at any minute. I could feel the sweat sliding down my back. How many eyes watching me were Vietcong? The sun had set. It was pitch dark, except for peoples' lighted homes or cooking fires. There were no streetlights.

Suddenly I was swarmed by about twelve children. "GI, you give me candy! GI, give me quarter!" They were tapping me and asking for treats and money. I was not prepared and my pockets were empty. "No have. No have... You go home now," was all I could say. Many sad faces turned away from me.

I got to the end of the street and asked an adult where the address I was looking for was located- and then waited. To my surprise, a man about 50 years old asked me why I was there. I said, "To visit this lady's family." I was then welcomed in and started my indoctrination into real Vietnamese culture, beliefs, and ways of doing things.

I became a regular in that neighborhood- going once a week to tutor the oldest son, who was 16 years old and getting ready to go to college. After class, I was allowed to visit with my friend for about half an hour. She could not speak to me until her father gave her permission. After I was "properly invited" to visit, the others pretended not to see me when I walked up the hill. Kids left me alone. If I made eye contact with an older person, I offered a small bow and received a bow back.

One day I asked my friend what the people thought of me.

"I am so glad you did not give anything to the children that first day," she told me. "People here hate Americans who turn our children into beggars. you would not have been welcomed if you had given them anything... but you were different than most other foreigners. The people here can't get over how brave you are. You came without a weapon and all alone."

"Is that unusual?" I asked.

"No white man has ever walked this street alone," she informed me.

"What about taxis?" I inquired.

"Must stay out, or may be shot," she replied.

Once again, I was left wondering How many Vietcong live among the people here?

My friend's father seemed to speak for the people of the street. Therefore, I thought he was the elder. Only the elder could give a man permission to "court" a daughter of the family. There came a day when I was told that the elder approved of me.

A week later, I was told by my command "Don't make any long term plans. We are pulling out soon." I sadly said my goodbyes. That was when I was introduced to the actual elder: the 80-year old mother of my friend's father. Upon seeing my surprise at discovering who she was, the elder smiled and informed me, "The elder is often a woman, especially in a country where men die young in war."

Night Shift And The Dog Handler

I met a security policeman with an unusual "Battle Buddy": a huge German shepherd police dog. The dog looked just like Rin Tin Tin, the famous canine movie star rescued from a World War I battlefield.

The two-legged soldier who worked with this dog was a nineteen-year-old sandy haired kid from somewhere in the Midwest. They were quite the team, these two. They patrolled at night between the inner and outer perimeter fence. One night, the policeman stopped to say "Hi" while I was on night shift and I offered him a cup of fresh coffee. That was the beginning of my friendship with the soldier and his dog. This was quite unique, since usually only the handler becomes a friend to an "attack dog." However, I got used to seeing those two in the middle of the night.

Then, one night when he stopped by, his face was pale and his hands were shaking.

"What's wrong?" I asked, noticing he was not smiling like he normally did.

"I thought my dog and I were going to die tonight!" He exclaimed. Then, coffee in hand, he told me his story:

It had been quiet for weeks. The soldier was getting used to "calm nights" ending with the dog not "alerting" and the perimeter being still. But that night, while making his rounds, the dog growled and his hair bristled. The dog's body language was a warning: Danger! Shocked, my friend then saw what the dog had detected: six zappers inside the outer perimeter fence with small arms and satchel charges.

He radioed for back-up, only to have the dispatcher order him to attack the Vietcong! It was one gun against six, but he cut his dog loose and ordered him to attack. The firefight was short and furious. My friend shot at muzzle blasts, which was all he could see since the Vietcong wore all black at night. When the enemy heard the dog's vicious growling and barking, they turned and ran while shooting over their shoulders at my friend and his dog. None of their bullets hit their targets. Every shot missed the dog and his handler.

These six zappers ran to a small lake on base where they dove under water and never resurfaced. The theory that circulated among the security police after this was that our enemy was using a "beaver hole" type of entrance in the bank somewhere that led to an underground tunnel or bunker. When my friend inspected the area where the enemy had run from, he didn't find any blood so he assumed that he had also missed his targets, despite the many bullets that had went flying during the firefight. It was his first enemy encounter and it had left him visibly shaken.

I don't know what happened to my friend. Shortly thereafter, I was transferred to another medical unit where he did not have access: a unit to "detox" American soldiers who were addicted to heroin. No visitors were allowed there.

THE HEROIN SMUGGLER

My last two months were spent as the only medic in the Heroin Rehab ward, a double locked, double gated area. All the soldiers residing there had tested positive for heroin and were now prisoners in a rehabilitation ward patrolled by a single armed guard. None were wounded. The prisoners were pending court martial and a dishonorable discharge. However, prior to appearing in a military court, they had to "dry out" first. As the medic assigned to this ward, it was my job to make sure they (medically) got through their detox period okay.

For most soldiers, it was a lot less painful to shoot heroin than to shoot yourself in the foot in order to get out of the war. I'd estimate that nine out of ten inmates only shot up once. Their goal: get discharged and live through the war. However, one out of ten of them was hard core addicted and had serious withdrawal symptoms.

There I was- locked in with about twenty inmates in a ward where no weapons were allowed. In a sense, that's actually kind of why I was there. Someone had recommended me to the Colonel as a possible medic for this ward because of my refusal to carry a weapon. The medic I was replacing had been beaten up, hogtied and gagged three times in one year- and all his inmates had escaped. I watched the medic shake and cry when the commander said he would have to go back if I refused. So, I "volunteered" under pressure. Everyone in the combat zone worked 12-hr days, six days per week, and I was given the night shift since that was when all the escapes had happened in the past.

My first few weeks went well. I had to show no fear, but I also had to enforce "the rules. I point blank told the inmates that if they touch me or break the rules they would go back to real jail. They knew what I meant: They would no longer have access to the air conditioning, good food, TV and movies they enjoyed in our ward. They would lose all the nice things about the unit. I told them to never threaten me, as I would not tolerate it.

One severely addicted man put me to the test. He demanded heroin. If I didn't produce what he wanted, he told me he was going to cut my throat. He spent the rest of his withdrawal in full restraints and the other prisoners saw that I meant what I said. However, when this addict was tested again 2 weeks later, his blood test showed his heroin level had gone up! Somebody was smuggling heroin into my ward...and the only people assigned to work here were guards and two medics (me and my daytime counterpart). So, I had my urine tested at least four times. I was getting frustrated. "Test the other guards and medic, please. It's not me!" I told my commander.

Meanwhile, I was watching like a hawk but never saw any heroin come into the ward. I found myself checking food trays and even the cart itself. I was really working hard to find how the drug was getting into the ward.

One night I was making my rounds when I stopped at the back door, which was barred and welded shut, to rest a bit. Lost in thought, I gazed off into the distance and saw movement from the corner of my eye. Turning, I glanced at the painted wooden door and saw something move in the center of the door. I silently moved closer to get a better look. Suddenly the image came into focus. It was the end of what looked like a hunting knife- moving in and out of the crack where the two doors met. Someone was outside carving a hole big enough to slip drug packets into my ward.

Got ya! I thought, silently retreating to the guard gate.

"Can you let me out, please?" I said loudly to the Security Policeman. "I need something from the surgical unit."

Before I exited the second door, I whispered to the guard "Please quietly call for back-up." I told him the smuggler was at the back door. Knowing this guard was forbidden to give me his sidearm, I quickly developed a plan.

"Just tell them to rush to the back door. I'll try to hold the person down until they get there," I told the guard. I was about to put myself against a person armed with a knife. Hopefully, just one person. Weeks of watchful waiting kindled the fire inside me that desperately wanted to see their faces. If it is just one person, I thought, I'll jump him. After all, I was trained in hand-to-hand combat, thanks to the Air Force Academy. Now it was time to use it. I saw a piece of 2x4 wood outside. It seemed just the right length, so I picked it up, arming myself. It was my only weapon, but I was not scared. I was angry- and determined to make the smuggling stop.

I went into "stalk" mode. Pretend it is a deer, I told myself. Make no sound at all. I walked silently and carefully. While it seemed like it took forever to get to the back corner of the building, it was actually just a few minutes. When I finally made it and peeked around the corner I saw... nobody. I could not see or hear anyone leaving the area. Wood in hand, I was ready to defend myself, but nobody came out of the darkness. I backed out and returned to the front gate just in time to meet back-up with the Security Police.

The smuggler had gotten away. But how did he know to run? Who told him? How did he know I was on my way?

48 hrs later I had a big shock! The guard who usually let me in had been replaced. The shock came when I saw him inside my unit in a prisoner uniform. I was immediately in his face. "You! My guard?" I spat. "How could you?"

Then he came clean and told me that as soon as I was out of sight, he had unlocked the inner door, ran to the back and told his helper to "Run like hell. Cope is on his way to kick your ass!"

The warning was given in vain, though. My command had agreed with me: Someone on the inside had warned the smuggler. So when this guard tested positive for heroin, it was the beginning of the end for both of them. They both ended up doing time in jail.

From that day, no heroin levels ever went back up in the prisoners. The commander really chewed my butt, though, for risking my life instead of letting the military cops do their job. The arrested guard gave up the rest of the drug ring. So the drug ring had been broken, but the commander still pleaded with me that day to "just be the medic in charge." I promised him I would.

The colonel put me in for a commendation medal for my work in the prisoner unit. His write up does not mention trying to apprehend the bad guys or helping to break a drug ring. Instead, he wrote something about doing a very difficult job, doing it well- and alone. It was a long and stressful two months that I spent in the heroin ward, but no prisoners escaped while I was on duty.

My assignment here ended when we pulled out of Vietnam. The war was over- for the Americans, at least.

IS THAT THE CHOW CART, MAN?

Trauma shapes and molds people. While the way people may react to trauma varies from person to person, trauma often scars the memory in such a way that it is hard to forget. This is one such story. Realizing that it may not sit well with some readers, I choose to still tell it here in hopes that you may better understand what we went through.

It was another day of rocket attacks. This time, I was on duty with the American heroin users in the "dry out" ward. I had just entered the area between the inner and outer locked doors of our double locked facility. I was going to man the gate for a few minutes while the guard used the restroom. That's when the siren sounded.

The ground vibrations and intensity of the blast sounds indicated that the rockets were hitting all around us. I ran back into the ward and made the inmates take cover. I then quickly slipped into my flack jacket and helmet and laid on the floor where I could watch the outer hall. Nobody moved. Then, I heard a gurney rolling down the hall. It stopped on the other side of the outer steel-framed door that was designed with a metal chain-link so that people could see through it.

Someone shouted on the other side of the door, "Leave the gurney for now. They need help with the other wounded outside!"

One of my prisoners had heard the sound of the rolling gurney from half way back and hollered, "Is that the chow cart, man?"

I yelled back, "No. Stay down."

The door opened up at the other end of the hall as the men who had been pushing the gurney ran out and an air gust blew the sheet off the head of the gurney. I gasped at what I saw. A staff sergeant was lying on the gurney. His bloodless, pale gray face hosted unseeing, open eyes that were fixed on the ceiling. Something dropped off the gurney onto the floor in front of me. My eyes began to focus on the image, just inches from my face. Watery, red fluid appeared before me, but there was also beige-pink globes of... something I couldn't quite make out. The puddle grew in size and my eyes followed the trail upward to see where it was coming from.

That's when I saw it. The left rear of the man's skull was missing. My stomach did a flip-flop as I realized that his brains were dripping onto the floor in front of me.

"Is that the chow cart, man?" the prisoner shouted again.

I gritted my teeth. I'd had enough. I hollered back, "For Christ's sake, would you shut the f*** up! They are not going to feed you during an attack!"

Later, I was ashamed of my choice of words, but I did get him to shut up. I also felt like crying. They couldn't see what was parked on the gurney-and I never told them. I found out later that the men outside the door had been pushing the gurney to the morgue located further down the hall.

I later heard the story of the man on the gurney: Two aircraft mechanics had gotten caught in the open, so they had decided to lie down, side-by-side, against the outside wall of the hanger. They had laid there, head to head, without any protective gear when a rocket suddenly hit just feet from them. When the man next to the building had risen and looked at his friend, declaring "Now that was close," his friend did not respond. Then he saw his staring eyes. He rolled him over to discover his friend's gaping head wound. The soldier that had survived did not even have a scratch on him. The soldier who had laid on the outside had taken all of the shrapnel.

The lost soldier left behind a wife and two kids who were back in the states. If only they had made it to a foxhole or inside of the building- they may have both survived that day. As the surviving soldier retold the story, he kept saying, "He shielded my body... and saved my life. He was my armor that day." The entire base mourned this soldier's sacrifice as the story of the two friends circulated the base. Their story stirred many to pray. None of us took our lives for granted.

UNIT PHOTO

We had a medical doctor as our commanding officer. He was a colonel who had over one hundred people under his command. When rumors started that we would be "pulling out" of Vietnam soon, he decided he wanted a unit photo as a keepsake. So he put up posters announcing where and when the photo would be.

One hundred people standing shoulder to shoulder- what a nice target that would be. How many civilian employees did we have? I wondered. How many could read English? What a perfect target for a bomb. Anyone who worked on base could pace out the yards to calculate a successful attack. All they would need to do is relay the coordinates to an enemy mortar or rocket crew... Needless to say, I was a bit scared!

I showed up a little over an hour early. I may just be a medic, but I wasn't about to be a passive target if I could help it. I checked under bench seats, in trash cans- anywhere I thought could be an easy place to conceal a bomb. I scoured the site for areas that looked like there may have been dirt disturbed recently. Then, I looked for possible areas of cover to hide in. I found nothing. I also did not see any other people doing what I was doing. There weren't even any security police around checking the area. There was nobody in sight. Great, I thought. Even with advanced advertising, there didn't seem to be any security in place.

I hope we survive. This was certainly something I would not do to my men if I was commanding in a combat zone! I'm not sure if it was a gutsy move or if there was little thought put into the decision. We certainly gave our enemy an easy target that day.

Fortunately, nothing happened- except for my commander revealing the only camera I ever saw after my first day in Vietnam. For most of us, cameras were confiscated as soon as we landed. Being caught with a camera was a court-martial offense that landed soldiers in prison. No one wanted photos of wounded getting back home and ending up on television.

My roommate, however, managed to keep his camera through his first day before surrendering it. I'm not sure how he managed that, but am grateful because the only photos I have of my time in Vietnam are the few he took in our houch that first day and one newspaper clipping that included a photo of me working with a patient. I had forgotten these photos even existed. I must have sent them to my parents with letters I wrote during my tour. Amazingly, my mother decided to keep the photos, even though there is no trace of any of the letters I wrote to her. I found the photos packed away in a shoebox with some other family photos around the time I began writing about my experiences in Vietnam. Up until then, I didn't have any photos of that time in my life. Other than those few photos, all I have are visions burned into my brain.

The lack of photos made me feel even more like a ghost when I came home. I would have to describe things so others could envision them, but nobody really wanted to hear about it. They were too busy trying to forget the war. They were tired of seeing it on the evening news everyday and were weary of the clash between those who wanted the United States out of the war and those who supported our government's desire to fight in the strangest places. So, we "ghosts" kept silent as our country hurried to forget the ten years of war. Shamed into silence, some of us even waited many years to even admit we were veterans of Vietnam. I found out years later that my parents did not even tell anyone where I was all those months. None of my high school classmates knew I was over there-and there are no letters from Vietnam in my father or mother's keepsakes, despite having written to them while there.

Years later, I hung a small flag with two bright yellow stars on it in my window in Texas because I had two children in combat zones: a son in Iraq and a daughter in Afghanistan. I still have that flag and will keep it until I die. When I displayed that flag, I wanted the world to know where my kids were and that I was proud but anxious for them. We were blessed in that both of them made it home without any physical wounds. They did not receive any purple heart medals either, which I was grateful for. The time they were away was the hardest I have ever prayed in my life. I prayed many times a day, every day. I could not watch the evening news; it always started with "Today in Bagdad..."

The evening news always made me remember how isolated we were when I was in combat. We were cut off from "real time" news broadcasts, so we only knew what the military wanted us to know. We survived on "rumors" which were usually pretty accurate. But, boy, were we in for a few shocks when we got home...

Leaving 'Nam

We all packed our duffle bags but placed two changes of civilian clothes in a smaller bag to carry with us on-board the aircraft as ordered. Then, another medic and I were chosen to take the gear over to the civilian airport to be put on the aircraft ahead of us. We used a completely empty ambulance to haul them over to the location just one block from the 3rd Army Field Hospital. We finished handing all the bags to the shipping clerk and climbed back into the ambulance when a shot rang out, very near to us. I took cover, hopping out of the vehicle and laying flat on the ground. I rolled under the ambulance for cover in case there was an elevated sniper.

Dead quiet followed. I took a big breath and shouted, "Who the hell is shooting?" No answer came, so I shouted it again.

A voice came from the jeep parked to the left of our ambulance, "I did."

I looked over at the army lieutenant as I got back into our vehicle. "What are you shooting at, Lieutenant?"

"Nothing! Shit...I accidentally shot myself."

I called for the other medic to come help me with the lieutenant who was sitting in the passenger seat of the other jeep.

"Where are you hit, sir?" I asked.

"In the middle of my left upper leg. I was cocking my .45 auto and when it closed, it fired."

Reaching for the weapon, I put it on safe mode. "It was on fire, sir, informed him. "You must have touched the trigger."

I checked his leg and found a small entry wound- and a much bigger exit wound. On the floor of the jeep I found a small piece of blood covered metal laying on the steel plate that was meant to stop land mine fragments. I picked up the slug and handed it to the lieutenant. He felt no pain and was not actively bleeding. We used a board and old rags to splint his leg in case the bone had fractured. We then got him to the nearby army hospital in five minutes flat.

The whole time, he kept saying, "My wife is going to kill me...all the way to 'Nam just to accidently shoot myself!" He seemed to be doing well when under our care, but I never saw him again after the incident. It was a bit weird. I never asked his name. We just addressed him by rank.

I was glad he was right-handed, though. Had he not been, that bullet could have hit me since he hadn't pointed the barrel in a safe direction. I could almost picture a movie actor cocking a .45 like that. Real life is so different from the movies. On screen, you see a lot of bad, unsafe weapon handling. I'd even seen my brother do unsafe things at home- and he's had weapons handling training. That didn't stop him from leaning on a rifle like Davy Crocket did on television though. Had his weapon gone off that day, the bullet would have gone through his hands and taken half his head and face off. My father came unglued when he saw him do it and threatened to take all of our guns away from us. From that day on, we determined we would not imitate stuff we see on television or in the movies... things like what the lieutenant did that day.

After the shooting incident on the runway, everything was fine for us until we loaded the civilian jetliner to fly home. Until the day I boarded that Plane, I did not even know that civilian aircraft have afterburners on their engines. We had only made it halfway down the runway for takeoff when I heard the engine "boom" like the afterburners were kicking in. The nose of the aircraft pitched up, almost vertically, and we pulled a lot of "G forces" as we were slammed back into our seats. I was sitting against a window as we took off. The sun had been setting as we boarded the aircraft, so by now it was Pretty dark outside. That made the color that appeared fairly easy to see. I saw lots of small red flashing lights on the end of the runway. Muzzle blasts, I thought. We had AK-47s and M-16s shooting at us from below. It appeared to be about thirty weapons firing at us. That's when I saw two bright yellow Streaks leave the ground and rapidly begin climbing towards our tail. It only took a split second for me to identify what I was seeing and think, The others should know.

I shouted as loud as I could, "Two stingers on the left!"

A man on the right window in my row shouted back, "One on the right!"

The aircraft got deafeningly silent except for the roar of the engines. I had trained to be able to fire stinger missiles at the United States Air Force Academy and I knew this was going to be close. Can we "outrun" three missiles fired from the shoulder of someone trying to bring us down? I thought. They're probably even South Vietnamese, angry about us leaving them behind. We only had seconds to pray. Then, I saw the two on the left side falling off towards the ground.

I shouted, "Okay on the left!"

The guy on the right side hollered, "Right side clear also!"

The plane erupted in an instant cheer. The entire aircraft went wild for a moment. We were enroute and finally going home. We had unlimited free alcohol during the flight. Everyone was in "party" mode. I joined them once a soldier I didn't know before the flight informed me that my missionary friend had finally left Saigon the day before we left. I had two beers to celebrate. I did not want to be drunk or hung-over when I got home.

We landed to refuel in Hawaii but were not allowed off of the aircraft. An hour from landing in San Francisco, we were ordered to change out of our uniforms into our civilian clothes. We were told to go to our next flight or proceed out of the airport as quickly as possible. We were ordered not to confront any protestors at the airport. We were instructed to just walk away from them.

"What protestors- and how many?" we wanted to know. No answers were given.

Getting off that plane was bizarre. Coming into the gate area, all I could see was a double row of riot-geared police holding back about 50-60 protestors. The protestors all had bags in their arms and large signs.

They were screaming at us. We were called many things, including "Baby Killers"- and much worse. Then they started throwing stuff over the riot police. We were getting pegged with rotten eggs and rotten vegetables. Thank God there were no rocks!

I covered my head with my outer arm and so did the soldier to my right. We trotted through "the gauntlet" and his eyes met mine.

"Holy Shit. We're under fire here more than we were in 'Nam!" I declared.

"Ain't this the shit," He replied. Then we got out of there.

When I saw myself in the mirror later, I understood why we were ordered to bring two sets of civilian clothes. I washed and changed so that my parents would not see me like this. I was not in the mood to talk much when I finally made it home to Pennsylvania. After de-boarding our first flight, we were all on different flights home. I didn't experience any more protestor assaults after that first one. Surely, this kind of behavior had to be illegal, but no arrests were made from what I could see.

Even though we were now home, we still couldn't tell our "friends" from our "enemies." We learned real quick to keep our mouths shut- and the isolation began.

THE AFTERMATH

A few months after I got home, I went to my Grandma Bish's annual 4th of July picnic. The food was excellent and I was enjoying being with my family until I overheard a male cousin of mine say in nearly a whisper, "Just watch what happens." Oh, no. What's he up to? I wondered. About ten minutes later I found out when a close loud "bang" exploded in my ears. Without thinking, I jumped forward, hit the ground and rolled three times. Then I looked for the "shooter," only to see my cousin and six other men laughing at me down on the ground. In his hand was the pieces of the paper bag he had "popped" right behind me.

I jumped up shouting, "You son of a bitch!" and he took off running with me close behind. It was not the first time he had done this to me. I caught up to him and put him down. With my left hand on his throat, and my right hand ready to smash his face, I shouted inches from his face "Either you stop doing this or I will beat the shit out of you until you do stop!"

I saw the fear in his eyes and I did not hit him. Nobody ever did that to me again either. The older men took him and the others aside and explained to them what they were doing to me. I heard one of them call me "shell shocked." As time went by, it got better. I eventually stopped leaping and rolling, but any loud noise still makes me want to drop low to the ground- even today.

THE RESCUE MISSION

I was working at the United States Air Force Academy Pediatric Unit when my "First Shirt," our senior ranking Sergeant, came to see me.

"They are asking for medics with time spent in 'Nam to go on a rescue mission," he informed me. "They want to empty out all the orphanages and bring the American children who are half American, half Vietnamese to the United States. They need medics to tend the children. There's about 300 of them. We're looking for volunteers to go."

"I need time to think and pray about it," I told him. "They tried to shoot us down when we left. How do we know they won't try again- even if we are loaded with kids?"

It took me an hour to decide. I sought the First Shirt out to tell him my decision.

"I'll go," I told him. "I wouldn't go back for anyone but the children though. I'll go for them." I had to admit to myself that I was still scared of being shot down.

"Sorry, Cope," he replied. "The flight is full. I got my last volunteer a half hour ago."

One week later, my First Shirt came to find me again. "You're not watching TV, are you?"

"At change of shift? I'm very busy. I never watch TV. What can I do for you, First Shirt?"

"You can sit down," he said.

"Can't we walk and talk, sir?" I asked. "I'm really quite busy."

"Cope, sit down right now! That's an order," he growled. So I did. He hesitated. "There's no easy way to say this... They are all dead- all of our medical staff on that mercy flight. Not a person on the flight crew survived. They crashed at take-off from Saigon."

I was stunned. "Sarge, Were they shot down?" I asked quietly.

"I don't know," he said. "Only three or four kids of the 330 on board survived. "

I was badly shaken. My hesitation and need to pray had saved my life, though I did not know why.

I researched it years later and for a time 747s and C5As were all grounded because of crashes on take-off. The cargo bay door was popping open due to electrical shorts in the wiring. The flight that crashed in Vietnam was probably #2 or #3 of the crashes. That problem has since been fixed, but what a relief it was to my soul to know that they had not been shot down. Yet, still a simple mechanical defect had taken the lives of many that day.

I never dreamed that anyone would ask me to go back to Vietnam. I met my future wife shortly after this sad mission failed. I do not doubt that God was indeed watching over me.

JUST FORGET IT EVER HAPPENED

I have a niece through marriage that shocked me. She heard one of my stories and realized that I still feel pain from my time in Vietnam.

"Uncle Dennis," she said. "Get over it. It is history. It happened more than 25 years ago. Just put it out of your mind and forget it ever happened."

Dear God, how I wish I could. Maybe that explains why I wrote my stories. I have accepted all of it- even understand the things that have shaped me into the person I am today because of it. Am I haunted by the past? Yes, to a degree.

I watched the United States tear itself apart over Vietnam. Now, I am part of its history. I went to see the "Traveling Wall," a small version of the Vietnam Memorial wall in Washington D.C. I have yet to see the big wall. The wall I saw brought me to tears. More than 58,000 fallen soldiers are honored on that wall. I even found one Copenhaver on that wall, but do not know him. It was a reminder to me of how grateful I am to have survived that war.

Today, when our troops are brought home, they are cheered and treated like heroes. The first time I saw this, I cried. The first time someone thanked me for my service in Vietnam, I cried again. I had returned home from the war 25 years earlier, but she was the first in all that time to thank me. What a journey my wartime service was- and it was just eight months of my life. Yet, it had such a profound effect on my life.

I've had people tell me, "You're the only Vietnam veteran I know who is normal." Perhaps that explains why I felt so isolated. Most people never even knew I went to Vietnam. I've heard recently about tours of Vietnam for Wartime veterans. From what I've heard, this can even help with the healing process. Just think: I may be able to tour the bunkers that were under my base if I ever go back. Even if I "get over it" one day... I doubt I will ever forget.

THE WAR THAT SAVED THE NEWLY WEDS

I returned from Vietnam in 1973. My wife, Cynthia, and I were married three years later. One year after our wedding, she was expecting our first child. One day we decided to hike along a mountain stream at the bottom of a deep ravine. The dam downstream was scheduled to close soon, and the stream we were hiking along would become the bottom of a lake when that happened. So, we'd decided to enjoy the area before the terrain was changed significantly. We noticed that a long bridge had already been constructed 1,000 feet above the streambed we were hiking alongside. We had hiked upstream during the afternoon and were returning just minutes before dark, so the canyon was now in deep shadow.

As we began to pass under the bridge, my wife grabbed my arm and She had heard a whistling noise that sounded like ducks whispered, "Ducks." landing with their wings set, a familiar sound to both of us as duck hunters. We both froze as we listened to the sound... then suddenly the pitch began to change and my mind recognized the noise as something else. My brain shrieked, "Incoming!" and my body reacted on instinct. It had been four years since my last attack in Vietnam and my automatic nervous system still went into action instantly. Without speaking or any conscious thought, my body reacted.

I grabbed Cynthia by her upper arm while tripping her. I threw her to the ground and threw my body on top of hers. She grunted as the wind was knocked out of her but before she could speak there was a terrific explosion along with a fireball that sent pieces of metal flying through the air. Something big and metallic had fallen from the bridge above, struck a large rock in the center of the creek about 15 yards from us and exploded. Pieces of metal had flown through the air and cut off three trees that were 4 to 5 inches in diameter and had just been cut 3 to 4 feet from the ground. Had we still been standing, we both would have been severely hurt or killed.

We stood up slowly and realized there were people on the bridge above us, laughing and rejoicing at the explosion! Realizing they had not seen us, I shouted at them. Startled, they took off running. They had just dropped a large metal acetylene fuel tank that is used in portable welding, in order to see it explode. It had broken open when it struck the rock and the sparks had ignited the fuel in the tank, creating a large bomb. Pieces had flown everywhere. They had not been trying to hurt us- they simply had not seen us!

Later, I thanked God for sparing us. I began to think, now you know why you had to go to war. You needed to learn to take cover instantly without pause... Had you not, you and your wife would have died. God used a traumatic event to train my reflexes so that we could survive- and it worked.

I had heard the falling rockets in Vietnam and known to take cover- and protect those I was with. I honestly did not have time to consciously think. I just reacted to that awful sound. It was the last time that I hit the ground in that way... so far.

LOOKING BACK

In closing this collection of stories, I realize that telling them has actually helped me put my entire experience into perspective. I can accept that the evils I saw exist in every war. So does the courage and the soldier's call to defend each other during life threatening situations. Today, I can tell my niece that my war is finally over. *I wonder if she will read my book? I hope she does in an effort to gain more understanding.*

For the most part, Vietnam vets were left to flounder on our own when we got home. Post-Traumatic Stress Disorder (PTSD) had not yet been described... but most of us definitely had it after seeing suffering or death. At the time there were no programs to help us release the internal stress of the experience. Most notable was the lack of anyone to talk to. Only a few of my close friends were Vietnam vets- and none of us were talking about our experiences in Vietnam. It took me years to even let people know that I was a Vietnam veteran. I simply heard too many people describe most Vietnam vets as either crazy or being on drugs or alcohol. It seemed that was how we were seen in the public eye. Therefore, it wasn't something I could declare with pride, so I kept it to myself.

We all knew that Americans at home were divided over the war. I do respect those who did everything they could to bring the war to a close. It disheartened me to see how Americans pitted themselves in protest against their own soldiers. I always felt that their protests should have been aimed at the government and politicians who controlled the military. I hope those reading this will remember that soldiers serve their country. They do not make the decisions to go to war but they do fight them. I feel Vietnam veterans deserve the same respect and admiration as all of our soldiers in other wars. We did not run away... We fought and risked death. We believed in our country and its principals. We even prayed for our leaders. I've even had General officers get down on their knees and pray with us! Today, I still pray for our government's leaders.

Now, in 2019, I've read in magazines and seen on television that there are now programs for Vietnam veterans to return to Vietnam to help them find healing. As I read about and watched these documentaries, I was flooded with a mixture of emotion. It was strange watching American soldiers meet old enemies and shake their hands. Some GIs got to tour the Vietcong tunnels that were under U.S. bases at the time of the war, which brought back my own memories of the tunnels and our enemy. Yet, how wonderful it was to see one Vietnam instead of a divided country. The beautiful countryside seems to be recovering under the rule of its communist government. Many of my clothes for the last 20 years have also had "Made in Vietnam" tags on them too- good quality clothes at competitive prices. I am certainly proud of the people there-I always was!

In 1982, our country finally honored our Vietnam veterans by dedicating the Vietnam memorial to the men and women who served in this controversial war. It was an excellent start. Now I think it is time for the silent warriors to tell their stories. My hope is that they will find healing in retelling their stories, just as I have. So, veterans, I am encouraging you to share your stories if you can. For all too soon, we too will fade away... and only our stories will remain.